GW01453113

Boat Log Book

COPYRIGHT © MATHIAS HEMINGWAY, 2020

THIS BOOK BELONGS TO:

CONTACT INFORMATION	
NAME:	
ADDRESS:	
PHONE:	

START / END DATES

_____ / ____ / ____   TO   _____ / ____ / ____

BOAT LOG AND RECORD

DATE		DESTINATION	
WEATHER		FORECAST	
WIND		VISIBILITY	
SEA CONDITIONS		ETA	

TIME	COURSE	SPEED	DISTANCE	NAVIGATION NOTES	REMARKS

EVENTS /OBSERVATIONS

TIME COMPLETED		DAYS RUN	
AVERAGE SPEED		FUEL ON BOARD	
CREW & GUESTS			
CAPTAIN			

BOAT LOG AND RECORD

DATE			DESTINATION	
WEATHER			FORECAST	
WIND			VISIBILITY	
SEA CONDITIONS			ETA	

TIME	COURSE	SPEED	DISTANCE	NAVIGATION NOTES	REMARKS

EVENTS /OBSERVATIONS

TIME COMPLETED		DAYS RUN	
AVERAGE SPEED		FUEL ON BOARD	
CREW & GUESTS			
CAPTAIN			

BOAT LOG AND RECORD

DATE		DESTINATION	
WEATHER		FORECAST	
WIND		VISIBILITY	
SEA CONDITIONS		ETA	

TIME	COURSE	SPEED	DISTANCE	NAVIGATION NOTES	REMARKS

EVENTS /OBSERVATIONS

TIME COMPLETED		DAYS RUN	
AVERAGE SPEED		FUEL ON BOARD	
CREW & GUESTS			

CAPTAIN	

BOAT LOG AND RECORD

DATE		DESTINATION	
WEATHER		FORECAST	
WIND		VISIBILITY	
SEA CONDITIONS		ETA	

TIME	COURSE	SPEED	DISTANCE	NAVIGATION NOTES	REMARKS

EVENTS /OBSERVATIONS

TIME COMPLETED		DAYS RUN	
AVERAGE SPEED		FUEL ON BOARD	
CREW & GUESTS			

CAPTAIN	

BOAT LOG AND RECORD

DATE		DESTINATION	
WEATHER		FORECAST	
WIND		VISIBILITY	
SEA CONDITIONS		ETA	

TIME	COURSE	SPEED	DISTANCE	NAVIGATION NOTES	REMARKS

EVENTS /OBSERVATIONS

TIME COMPLETED		DAYS RUN	
AVERAGE SPEED		FUEL ON BOARD	
CREW & GUESTS			
CAPTAIN			

BOAT LOG AND RECORD

DATE		DESTINATION	
WEATHER		FORECAST	
WIND		VISIBILITY	
SEA CONDITIONS		ETA	

TIME	COURSE	SPEED	DISTANCE	NAVIGATION NOTES	REMARKS

EVENTS /OBSERVATIONS

TIME COMPLETED		DAYS RUN	
AVERAGE SPEED		FUEL ON BOARD	
CREW & GUESTS			
CAPTAIN			

BOAT LOG AND RECORD

DATE		DESTINATION	
WEATHER		FORECAST	
WIND		VISIBILITY	
SEA CONDITIONS		ETA	

TIME	COURSE	SPEED	DISTANCE	NAVIGATION NOTES	REMARKS

EVENTS /OBSERVATIONS

TIME COMPLETED		DAYS RUN	
AVERAGE SPEED		FUEL ON BOARD	
CREW & GUESTS			

CAPTAIN	

BOAT LOG AND RECORD

DATE			DESTINATION	
WEATHER			FORECAST	
WIND			VISIBILITY	
SEA CONDITIONS			ETA	

TIME	COURSE	SPEED	DISTANCE	NAVIGATION NOTES	REMARKS

EVENTS /OBSERVATIONS

TIME COMPLETED		DAYS RUN	
AVERAGE SPEED		FUEL ON BOARD	
CREW & GUESTS			
CAPTAIN			

BOAT LOG AND RECORD

DATE		DESTINATION	
WEATHER		FORECAST	
WIND		VISIBILITY	
SEA CONDITIONS		ETA	

TIME	COURSE	SPEED	DISTANCE	NAVIGATION NOTES	REMARKS

EVENTS /OBSERVATIONS

TIME COMPLETED		DAYS RUN	
AVERAGE SPEED		FUEL ON BOARD	
CREW & GUESTS			

CAPTAIN	

BOAT LOG AND RECORD

DATE		DESTINATION	
WEATHER		FORECAST	
WIND		VISIBILITY	
SEA CONDITIONS		ETA	

TIME	COURSE	SPEED	DISTANCE	NAVIGATION NOTES	REMARKS

EVENTS /OBSERVATIONS

TIME COMPLETED		DAYS RUN	
AVERAGE SPEED		FUEL ON BOARD	
CREW & GUESTS			

CAPTAIN	

BOAT LOG AND RECORD

DATE		DESTINATION	
WEATHER		FORECAST	
WIND		VISIBILITY	
SEA CONDITIONS		ETA	

TIME	COURSE	SPEED	DISTANCE	NAVIGATION NOTES	REMARKS

EVENTS /OBSERVATIONS

TIME COMPLETED		DAYS RUN	
AVERAGE SPEED		FUEL ON BOARD	
CREW & GUESTS			

CAPTAIN	

BOAT LOG AND RECORD

DATE		DESTINATION	
WEATHER		FORECAST	
WIND		VISIBILITY	
SEA CONDITIONS		ETA	

TIME	COURSE	SPEED	DISTANCE	NAVIGATION NOTES	REMARKS

EVENTS /OBSERVATIONS

TIME COMPLETED		DAYS RUN	
AVERAGE SPEED		FUEL ON BOARD	
CREW & GUESTS			

CAPTAIN	

BOAT LOG AND RECORD

DATE		DESTINATION	
WEATHER		FORECAST	
WIND		VISIBILITY	
SEA CONDITIONS		ETA	

TIME	COURSE	SPEED	DISTANCE	NAVIGATION NOTES	REMARKS

EVENTS /OBSERVATIONS

TIME COMPLETED		DAYS RUN	
AVERAGE SPEED		FUEL ON BOARD	
CREW & GUESTS			
CAPTAIN			

BOAT LOG AND RECORD

DATE		DESTINATION	
WEATHER		FORECAST	
WIND		VISIBILITY	
SEA CONDITIONS		ETA	

TIME	COURSE	SPEED	DISTANCE	NAVIGATION NOTES	REMARKS

EVENTS /OBSERVATIONS

TIME COMPLETED		DAYS RUN	
AVERAGE SPEED		FUEL ON BOARD	
CREW & GUESTS			

CAPTAIN	

BOAT LOG AND RECORD

DATE		DESTINATION	
WEATHER		FORECAST	
WIND		VISIBILITY	
SEA CONDITIONS		ETA	

TIME	COURSE	SPEED	DISTANCE	NAVIGATION NOTES	REMARKS

EVENTS /OBSERVATIONS

TIME COMPLETED		DAYS RUN	
AVERAGE SPEED		FUEL ON BOARD	
CREW & GUESTS			
CAPTAIN			

BOAT LOG AND RECORD

DATE		DESTINATION	
WEATHER		FORECAST	
WIND		VISIBILITY	
SEA CONDITIONS		ETA	

TIME	COURSE	SPEED	DISTANCE	NAVIGATION NOTES	REMARKS

EVENTS /OBSERVATIONS

TIME COMPLETED		DAYS RUN	
AVERAGE SPEED		FUEL ON BOARD	
CREW & GUESTS			

CAPTAIN	

BOAT LOG AND RECORD

DATE		DESTINATION	
WEATHER		FORECAST	
WIND		VISIBILITY	
SEA CONDITIONS		ETA	

TIME	COURSE	SPEED	DISTANCE	NAVIGATION NOTES	REMARKS

EVENTS /OBSERVATIONS

TIME COMPLETED		DAYS RUN	
AVERAGE SPEED		FUEL ON BOARD	
CREW & GUESTS			
CAPTAIN			

BOAT LOG AND RECORD

DATE		DESTINATION	
WEATHER		FORECAST	
WIND		VISIBILITY	
SEA CONDITIONS		ETA	

TIME	COURSE	SPEED	DISTANCE	NAVIGATION NOTES	REMARKS

EVENTS /OBSERVATIONS

TIME COMPLETED		DAYS RUN	
AVERAGE SPEED		FUEL ON BOARD	

CREW & GUESTS	

CAPTAIN	

BOAT LOG AND RECORD

DATE		DESTINATION	
WEATHER		FORECAST	
WIND		VISIBILITY	
SEA CONDITIONS		ETA	

TIME	COURSE	SPEED	DISTANCE	NAVIGATION NOTES	REMARKS

EVENTS /OBSERVATIONS

TIME COMPLETED		DAYS RUN	
AVERAGE SPEED		FUEL ON BOARD	
CREW & GUESTS			
CAPTAIN			

BOAT LOG AND RECORD

DATE		DESTINATION	
WEATHER		FORECAST	
WIND		VISIBILITY	
SEA CONDITIONS		ETA	

TIME	COURSE	SPEED	DISTANCE	NAVIGATION NOTES	REMARKS

EVENTS /OBSERVATIONS

TIME COMPLETED		DAYS RUN	
AVERAGE SPEED		FUEL ON BOARD	
CREW & GUESTS			
CAPTAIN			

BOAT LOG AND RECORD

DATE		DESTINATION	
WEATHER		FORECAST	
WIND		VISIBILITY	
SEA CONDITIONS		ETA	

TIME	COURSE	SPEED	DISTANCE	NAVIGATION NOTES	REMARKS

EVENTS /OBSERVATIONS

TIME COMPLETED		DAYS RUN	
AVERAGE SPEED		FUEL ON BOARD	
CREW & GUESTS			

CAPTAIN	

BOAT LOG AND RECORD

DATE		DESTINATION	
WEATHER		FORECAST	
WIND		VISIBILITY	
SEA CONDITIONS		ETA	

TIME	COURSE	SPEED	DISTANCE	NAVIGATION NOTES	REMARKS

EVENTS /OBSERVATIONS

TIME COMPLETED		DAYS RUN	
AVERAGE SPEED		FUEL ON BOARD	
CREW & GUESTS			
CAPTAIN			

BOAT LOG AND RECORD

DATE		DESTINATION	
WEATHER		FORECAST	
WIND		VISIBILITY	
SEA CONDITIONS		ETA	

TIME	COURSE	SPEED	DISTANCE	NAVIGATION NOTES	REMARKS

EVENTS /OBSERVATIONS

TIME COMPLETED		DAYS RUN	
AVERAGE SPEED		FUEL ON BOARD	
CREW & GUESTS			

CAPTAIN	

BOAT LOG AND RECORD

DATE		DESTINATION	
WEATHER		FORECAST	
WIND		VISIBILITY	
SEA CONDITIONS		ETA	

TIME	COURSE	SPEED	DISTANCE	NAVIGATION NOTES	REMARKS

EVENTS /OBSERVATIONS

TIME COMPLETED		DAYS RUN	
AVERAGE SPEED		FUEL ON BOARD	
CREW & GUESTS			

CAPTAIN	

BOAT LOG AND RECORD

DATE			DESTINATION	
WEATHER			FORECAST	
WIND			VISIBILITY	
SEA CONDITIONS			ETA	

TIME	COURSE	SPEED	DISTANCE	NAVIGATION NOTES	REMARKS

EVENTS /OBSERVATIONS

TIME COMPLETED			DAYS RUN	
AVERAGE SPEED			FUEL ON BOARD	
CREW & GUESTS				
CAPTAIN				

BOAT LOG AND RECORD

DATE		DESTINATION	
WEATHER		FORECAST	
WIND		VISIBILITY	
SEA CONDITIONS		ETA	

TIME	COURSE	SPEED	DISTANCE	NAVIGATION NOTES	REMARKS

EVENTS /OBSERVATIONS

TIME COMPLETED		DAYS RUN	
AVERAGE SPEED		FUEL ON BOARD	
CREW & GUESTS			

CAPTAIN	

BOAT LOG AND RECORD

DATE		DESTINATION	
WEATHER		FORECAST	
WIND		VISIBILITY	
SEA CONDITIONS		ETA	

TIME	COURSE	SPEED	DISTANCE	NAVIGATION NOTES	REMARKS

EVENTS /OBSERVATIONS

TIME COMPLETED		DAYS RUN	
AVERAGE SPEED		FUEL ON BOARD	
CREW & GUESTS			

CAPTAIN	

BOAT LOG AND RECORD

DATE		DESTINATION	
WEATHER		FORECAST	
WIND		VISIBILITY	
SEA CONDITIONS		ETA	

TIME	COURSE	SPEED	DISTANCE	NAVIGATION NOTES	REMARKS

EVENTS /OBSERVATIONS

TIME COMPLETED		DAYS RUN	
AVERAGE SPEED		FUEL ON BOARD	
CREW & GUESTS			

CAPTAIN	

BOAT LOG AND RECORD

DATE		DESTINATION	
WEATHER		FORECAST	
WIND		VISIBILITY	
SEA CONDITIONS		ETA	

TIME	COURSE	SPEED	DISTANCE	NAVIGATION NOTES	REMARKS

EVENTS /OBSERVATIONS

TIME COMPLETED		DAYS RUN	
AVERAGE SPEED		FUEL ON BOARD	

CREW & GUESTS	

CAPTAIN	

BOAT LOG AND RECORD

DATE		DESTINATION	
WEATHER		FORECAST	
WIND		VISIBILITY	
SEA CONDITIONS		ETA	

TIME	COURSE	SPEED	DISTANCE	NAVIGATION NOTES	REMARKS

EVENTS /OBSERVATIONS

TIME COMPLETED		DAYS RUN	
AVERAGE SPEED		FUEL ON BOARD	
CREW & GUESTS			
CAPTAIN			

BOAT LOG AND RECORD

DATE		DESTINATION	
WEATHER		FORECAST	
WIND		VISIBILITY	
SEA CONDITIONS		ETA	

TIME	COURSE	SPEED	DISTANCE	NAVIGATION NOTES	REMARKS

EVENTS /OBSERVATIONS

TIME COMPLETED		DAYS RUN	
AVERAGE SPEED		FUEL ON BOARD	
CREW & GUESTS			

CAPTAIN	

BOAT LOG AND RECORD

DATE		DESTINATION	
WEATHER		FORECAST	
WIND		VISIBILITY	
SEA CONDITIONS		ETA	

TIME	COURSE	SPEED	DISTANCE	NAVIGATION NOTES	REMARKS

EVENTS /OBSERVATIONS

TIME COMPLETED		DAYS RUN	
AVERAGE SPEED		FUEL ON BOARD	
CREW & GUESTS			
CAPTAIN			

BOAT LOG AND RECORD

DATE		DESTINATION	
WEATHER		FORECAST	
WIND		VISIBILITY	
SEA CONDITIONS		ETA	

TIME	COURSE	SPEED	DISTANCE	NAVIGATION NOTES	REMARKS

EVENTS /OBSERVATIONS

TIME COMPLETED		DAYS RUN	
AVERAGE SPEED		FUEL ON BOARD	
CREW & GUESTS			
CAPTAIN			

BOAT LOG AND RECORD

DATE		DESTINATION	
WEATHER		FORECAST	
WIND		VISIBILITY	
SEA CONDITIONS		ETA	

TIME	COURSE	SPEED	DISTANCE	NAVIGATION NOTES	REMARKS

EVENTS /OBSERVATIONS

TIME COMPLETED		DAYS RUN	
AVERAGE SPEED		FUEL ON BOARD	
CREW & GUESTS			

CAPTAIN	

BOAT LOG AND RECORD

DATE		DESTINATION	
WEATHER		FORECAST	
WIND		VISIBILITY	
SEA CONDITIONS		ETA	

TIME	COURSE	SPEED	DISTANCE	NAVIGATION NOTES	REMARKS

EVENTS /OBSERVATIONS

TIME COMPLETED		DAYS RUN	
AVERAGE SPEED		FUEL ON BOARD	
CREW & GUESTS			

CAPTAIN	

BOAT LOG AND RECORD

DATE		DESTINATION	
WEATHER		FORECAST	
WIND		VISIBILITY	
SEA CONDITIONS		ETA	

TIME	COURSE	SPEED	DISTANCE	NAVIGATION NOTES	REMARKS

EVENTS /OBSERVATIONS

TIME COMPLETED		DAYS RUN	
AVERAGE SPEED		FUEL ON BOARD	
CREW & GUESTS			
CAPTAIN			

BOAT LOG AND RECORD

DATE		DESTINATION	
WEATHER		FORECAST	
WIND		VISIBILITY	
SEA CONDITIONS		ETA	

TIME	COURSE	SPEED	DISTANCE	NAVIGATION NOTES	REMARKS

EVENTS /OBSERVATIONS

TIME COMPLETED		DAYS RUN	
AVERAGE SPEED		FUEL ON BOARD	
CREW & GUESTS			
CAPTAIN			

BOAT LOG AND RECORD

DATE		DESTINATION	
WEATHER		FORECAST	
WIND		VISIBILITY	
SEA CONDITIONS		ETA	

TIME	COURSE	SPEED	DISTANCE	NAVIGATION NOTES	REMARKS

EVENTS /OBSERVATIONS

TIME COMPLETED		DAYS RUN	
AVERAGE SPEED		FUEL ON BOARD	
CREW & GUESTS			
CAPTAIN			

BOAT LOG AND RECORD

DATE		DESTINATION	
WEATHER		FORECAST	
WIND		VISIBILITY	
SEA CONDITIONS		ETA	

TIME	COURSE	SPEED	DISTANCE	NAVIGATION NOTES	REMARKS

EVENTS /OBSERVATIONS

TIME COMPLETED		DAYS RUN	
AVERAGE SPEED		FUEL ON BOARD	
CREW & GUESTS			

CAPTAIN	

BOAT LOG AND RECORD

DATE		DESTINATION	
WEATHER		FORECAST	
WIND		VISIBILITY	
SEA CONDITIONS		ETA	

TIME	COURSE	SPEED	DISTANCE	NAVIGATION NOTES	REMARKS

EVENTS /OBSERVATIONS

TIME COMPLETED		DAYS RUN	
AVERAGE SPEED		FUEL ON BOARD	
CREW & GUESTS			

CAPTAIN	

BOAT LOG AND RECORD

DATE			DESTINATION	
WEATHER			FORECAST	
WIND			VISIBILITY	
SEA CONDITIONS			ETA	

TIME	COURSE	SPEED	DISTANCE	NAVIGATION NOTES	REMARKS

EVENTS /OBSERVATIONS

TIME COMPLETED			DAYS RUN	
AVERAGE SPEED			FUEL ON BOARD	
CREW & GUESTS				
CAPTAIN				

BOAT LOG AND RECORD

DATE		DESTINATION	
WEATHER		FORECAST	
WIND		VISIBILITY	
SEA CONDITIONS		ETA	

TIME	COURSE	SPEED	DISTANCE	NAVIGATION NOTES	REMARKS

EVENTS /OBSERVATIONS

TIME COMPLETED		DAYS RUN	
AVERAGE SPEED		FUEL ON BOARD	
CREW & GUESTS			
CAPTAIN			

BOAT LOG AND RECORD

DATE		DESTINATION	
WEATHER		FORECAST	
WIND		VISIBILITY	
SEA CONDITIONS		ETA	

TIME	COURSE	SPEED	DISTANCE	NAVIGATION NOTES	REMARKS

EVENTS /OBSERVATIONS

TIME COMPLETED		DAYS RUN	
AVERAGE SPEED		FUEL ON BOARD	
CREW & GUESTS			
CAPTAIN			

BOAT LOG AND RECORD

DATE		DESTINATION	
WEATHER		FORECAST	
WIND		VISIBILITY	
SEA CONDITIONS		ETA	

TIME	COURSE	SPEED	DISTANCE	NAVIGATION NOTES	REMARKS

EVENTS /OBSERVATIONS

TIME COMPLETED		DAYS RUN	
AVERAGE SPEED		FUEL ON BOARD	
CREW & GUESTS			
CAPTAIN			

BOAT LOG AND RECORD

DATE		DESTINATION	
WEATHER		FORECAST	
WIND		VISIBILITY	
SEA CONDITIONS		ETA	

TIME	COURSE	SPEED	DISTANCE	NAVIGATION NOTES	REMARKS

EVENTS /OBSERVATIONS

TIME COMPLETED		DAYS RUN	
AVERAGE SPEED		FUEL ON BOARD	
CREW & GUESTS			

CAPTAIN	

BOAT LOG AND RECORD

DATE		DESTINATION	
WEATHER		FORECAST	
WIND		VISIBILITY	
SEA CONDITIONS		ETA	

TIME	COURSE	SPEED	DISTANCE	NAVIGATION NOTES	REMARKS

EVENTS /OBSERVATIONS

TIME COMPLETED		DAYS RUN	
AVERAGE SPEED		FUEL ON BOARD	
CREW & GUESTS			
CAPTAIN			

BOAT LOG AND RECORD

DATE		DESTINATION	
WEATHER		FORECAST	
WIND		VISIBILITY	
SEA CONDITIONS		ETA	

TIME	COURSE	SPEED	DISTANCE	NAVIGATION NOTES	REMARKS

EVENTS /OBSERVATIONS

TIME COMPLETED		DAYS RUN	
AVERAGE SPEED		FUEL ON BOARD	

CREW & GUESTS	

CAPTAIN	

BOAT LOG AND RECORD

DATE		DESTINATION	
WEATHER		FORECAST	
WIND		VISIBILITY	
SEA CONDITIONS		ETA	

TIME	COURSE	SPEED	DISTANCE	NAVIGATION NOTES	REMARKS

EVENTS /OBSERVATIONS

TIME COMPLETED		DAYS RUN	
AVERAGE SPEED		FUEL ON BOARD	
CREW & GUESTS			
CAPTAIN			

BOAT LOG AND RECORD

DATE		DESTINATION	
WEATHER		FORECAST	
WIND		VISIBILITY	
SEA CONDITIONS		ETA	

TIME	COURSE	SPEED	DISTANCE	NAVIGATION NOTES	REMARKS

EVENTS /OBSERVATIONS

TIME COMPLETED		DAYS RUN		
AVERAGE SPEED		FUEL ON BOARD		
CREW & GUESTS				
CAPTAIN				

BOAT LOG AND RECORD

DATE		DESTINATION	
WEATHER		FORECAST	
WIND		VISIBILITY	
SEA CONDITIONS		ETA	

TIME	COURSE	SPEED	DISTANCE	NAVIGATION NOTES	REMARKS

EVENTS /OBSERVATIONS

TIME COMPLETED		DAYS RUN	
AVERAGE SPEED		FUEL ON BOARD	
CREW & GUESTS			
CAPTAIN			

BOAT LOG AND RECORD

DATE		DESTINATION	
WEATHER		FORECAST	
WIND		VISIBILITY	
SEA CONDITIONS		ETA	

TIME	COURSE	SPEED	DISTANCE	NAVIGATION NOTES	REMARKS

EVENTS /OBSERVATIONS

TIME COMPLETED		DAYS RUN	
AVERAGE SPEED		FUEL ON BOARD	
CREW & GUESTS			

CAPTAIN	

BOAT LOG AND RECORD

DATE		DESTINATION	
WEATHER		FORECAST	
WIND		VISIBILITY	
SEA CONDITIONS		ETA	

TIME	COURSE	SPEED	DISTANCE	NAVIGATION NOTES	REMARKS

EVENTS /OBSERVATIONS

TIME COMPLETED		DAYS RUN	
AVERAGE SPEED		FUEL ON BOARD	
CREW & GUESTS			
CAPTAIN			

BOAT LOG AND RECORD

DATE		DESTINATION	
WEATHER		FORECAST	
WIND		VISIBILITY	
SEA CONDITIONS		ETA	

TIME	COURSE	SPEED	DISTANCE	NAVIGATION NOTES	REMARKS

EVENTS /OBSERVATIONS

TIME COMPLETED		DAYS RUN	
AVERAGE SPEED		FUEL ON BOARD	
CREW & GUESTS			
CAPTAIN			

BOAT LOG AND RECORD

DATE		DESTINATION	
WEATHER		FORECAST	
WIND		VISIBILITY	
SEA CONDITIONS		ETA	

TIME	COURSE	SPEED	DISTANCE	NAVIGATION NOTES	REMARKS

EVENTS /OBSERVATIONS

TIME COMPLETED		DAYS RUN	
AVERAGE SPEED		FUEL ON BOARD	
CREW & GUESTS			
CAPTAIN			

BOAT LOG AND RECORD

DATE		DESTINATION	
WEATHER		FORECAST	
WIND		VISIBILITY	
SEA CONDITIONS		ETA	

TIME	COURSE	SPEED	DISTANCE	NAVIGATION NOTES	REMARKS

EVENTS /OBSERVATIONS

TIME COMPLETED		DAYS RUN	
AVERAGE SPEED		FUEL ON BOARD	
CREW & GUESTS			
CAPTAIN			

BOAT LOG AND RECORD

DATE		DESTINATION	
WEATHER		FORECAST	
WIND		VISIBILITY	
SEA CONDITIONS		ETA	

TIME	COURSE	SPEED	DISTANCE	NAVIGATION NOTES	REMARKS

EVENTS /OBSERVATIONS

TIME COMPLETED		DAYS RUN	
AVERAGE SPEED		FUEL ON BOARD	
CREW & GUESTS			
CAPTAIN			

BOAT LOG AND RECORD

DATE		DESTINATION	
WEATHER		FORECAST	
WIND		VISIBILITY	
SEA CONDITIONS		ETA	

TIME	COURSE	SPEED	DISTANCE	NAVIGATION NOTES	REMARKS

EVENTS /OBSERVATIONS

TIME COMPLETED		DAYS RUN	
AVERAGE SPEED		FUEL ON BOARD	
CREW & GUESTS			

CAPTAIN	

BOAT LOG AND RECORD

DATE		DESTINATION	
WEATHER		FORECAST	
WIND		VISIBILITY	
SEA CONDITIONS		ETA	

TIME	COURSE	SPEED	DISTANCE	NAVIGATION NOTES	REMARKS

EVENTS /OBSERVATIONS

TIME COMPLETED		DAYS RUN	
AVERAGE SPEED		FUEL ON BOARD	
CREW & GUESTS			

CAPTAIN	

BOAT LOG AND RECORD

DATE			DESTINATION	
WEATHER			FORECAST	
WIND			VISIBILITY	
SEA CONDITIONS			ETA	

TIME	COURSE	SPEED	DISTANCE	NAVIGATION NOTES	REMARKS

EVENTS /OBSERVATIONS

TIME COMPLETED		DAYS RUN	
AVERAGE SPEED		FUEL ON BOARD	
CREW & GUESTS			
CAPTAIN			

BOAT LOG AND RECORD

DATE		DESTINATION	
WEATHER		FORECAST	
WIND		VISIBILITY	
SEA CONDITIONS		ETA	

TIME	COURSE	SPEED	DISTANCE	NAVIGATION NOTES	REMARKS

EVENTS /OBSERVATIONS

TIME COMPLETED		DAYS RUN	
AVERAGE SPEED		FUEL ON BOARD	
CREW & GUESTS			
CAPTAIN			

BOAT LOG AND RECORD

DATE		DESTINATION	
WEATHER		FORECAST	
WIND		VISIBILITY	
SEA CONDITIONS		ETA	

TIME	COURSE	SPEED	DISTANCE	NAVIGATION NOTES	REMARKS

EVENTS /OBSERVATIONS

TIME COMPLETED		DAYS RUN	
AVERAGE SPEED		FUEL ON BOARD	
CREW & GUESTS			
CAPTAIN			

BOAT LOG AND RECORD

DATE		DESTINATION	
WEATHER		FORECAST	
WIND		VISIBILITY	
SEA CONDITIONS		ETA	

TIME	COURSE	SPEED	DISTANCE	NAVIGATION NOTES	REMARKS

EVENTS /OBSERVATIONS

TIME COMPLETED		DAYS RUN	
AVERAGE SPEED		FUEL ON BOARD	
CREW & GUESTS			
CAPTAIN			

BOAT LOG AND RECORD

DATE		DESTINATION	
WEATHER		FORECAST	
WIND		VISIBILITY	
SEA CONDITIONS		ETA	

TIME	COURSE	SPEED	DISTANCE	NAVIGATION NOTES	REMARKS

EVENTS /OBSERVATIONS

TIME COMPLETED		DAYS RUN	
AVERAGE SPEED		FUEL ON BOARD	
CREW & GUESTS			

CAPTAIN	

BOAT LOG AND RECORD

DATE		DESTINATION	
WEATHER		FORECAST	
WIND		VISIBILITY	
SEA CONDITIONS		ETA	

TIME	COURSE	SPEED	DISTANCE	NAVIGATION NOTES	REMARKS

EVENTS /OBSERVATIONS

TIME COMPLETED		DAYS RUN	
AVERAGE SPEED		FUEL ON BOARD	

CREW & GUESTS	

CAPTAIN	

BOAT LOG AND RECORD

DATE		DESTINATION	
WEATHER		FORECAST	
WIND		VISIBILITY	
SEA CONDITIONS		ETA	

TIME	COURSE	SPEED	DISTANCE	NAVIGATION NOTES	REMARKS

EVENTS /OBSERVATIONS

TIME COMPLETED		DAYS RUN	
AVERAGE SPEED		FUEL ON BOARD	
CREW & GUESTS			
CAPTAIN			

BOAT LOG AND RECORD

DATE		DESTINATION	
WEATHER		FORECAST	
WIND		VISIBILITY	
SEA CONDITIONS		ETA	

TIME	COURSE	SPEED	DISTANCE	NAVIGATION NOTES	REMARKS

EVENTS /OBSERVATIONS

TIME COMPLETED		DAYS RUN	
AVERAGE SPEED		FUEL ON BOARD	
CREW & GUESTS			
CAPTAIN			

BOAT LOG AND RECORD

DATE		DESTINATION	
WEATHER		FORECAST	
WIND		VISIBILITY	
SEA CONDITIONS		ETA	

TIME	COURSE	SPEED	DISTANCE	NAVIGATION NOTES	REMARKS

EVENTS /OBSERVATIONS

TIME COMPLETED		DAYS RUN	
AVERAGE SPEED		FUEL ON BOARD	
CREW & GUESTS			
CAPTAIN			

BOAT LOG AND RECORD

DATE		DESTINATION	
WEATHER		FORECAST	
WIND		VISIBILITY	
SEA CONDITIONS		ETA	

TIME	COURSE	SPEED	DISTANCE	NAVIGATION NOTES	REMARKS

EVENTS /OBSERVATIONS

TIME COMPLETED		DAYS RUN	
AVERAGE SPEED		FUEL ON BOARD	
CREW & GUESTS			

CAPTAIN	

BOAT LOG AND RECORD

DATE		DESTINATION	
WEATHER		FORECAST	
WIND		VISIBILITY	
SEA CONDITIONS		ETA	

TIME	COURSE	SPEED	DISTANCE	NAVIGATION NOTES	REMARKS

EVENTS /OBSERVATIONS

TIME COMPLETED		DAYS RUN	
AVERAGE SPEED		FUEL ON BOARD	
CREW & GUESTS			
CAPTAIN			

BOAT LOG AND RECORD

DATE		DESTINATION	
WEATHER		FORECAST	
WIND		VISIBILITY	
SEA CONDITIONS		ETA	

TIME	COURSE	SPEED	DISTANCE	NAVIGATION NOTES	REMARKS

EVENTS /OBSERVATIONS

TIME COMPLETED		DAYS RUN	
AVERAGE SPEED		FUEL ON BOARD	
CREW & GUESTS			

CAPTAIN	

BOAT LOG AND RECORD

DATE		DESTINATION	
WEATHER		FORECAST	
WIND		VISIBILITY	
SEA CONDITIONS		ETA	

TIME	COURSE	SPEED	DISTANCE	NAVIGATION NOTES	REMARKS

EVENTS /OBSERVATIONS

TIME COMPLETED		DAYS RUN	
AVERAGE SPEED		FUEL ON BOARD	
CREW & GUESTS			

CAPTAIN	

BOAT LOG AND RECORD

DATE		DESTINATION	
WEATHER		FORECAST	
WIND		VISIBILITY	
SEA CONDITIONS		ETA	

TIME	COURSE	SPEED	DISTANCE	NAVIGATION NOTES	REMARKS

EVENTS /OBSERVATIONS

TIME COMPLETED		DAYS RUN	
AVERAGE SPEED		FUEL ON BOARD	
CREW & GUESTS			
CAPTAIN			

BOAT LOG AND RECORD

DATE		DESTINATION	
WEATHER		FORECAST	
WIND		VISIBILITY	
SEA CONDITIONS		ETA	

TIME	COURSE	SPEED	DISTANCE	NAVIGATION NOTES	REMARKS

EVENTS /OBSERVATIONS

TIME COMPLETED		DAYS RUN		
AVERAGE SPEED		FUEL ON BOARD		
CREW & GUESTS				
CAPTAIN				

BOAT LOG AND RECORD

DATE		DESTINATION	
WEATHER		FORECAST	
WIND		VISIBILITY	
SEA CONDITIONS		ETA	

TIME	COURSE	SPEED	DISTANCE	NAVIGATION NOTES	REMARKS

EVENTS /OBSERVATIONS

TIME COMPLETED		DAYS RUN	
AVERAGE SPEED		FUEL ON BOARD	
CREW & GUESTS			

CAPTAIN	

BOAT/MOTOR MAINTENANCE

BOAT MAKE		MODEL			
YEAR		HIN			
MOTOR MAKE		MODEL		SERIAL #	

DATE (MM/DD/YY)	ENGINE HOURS (P/S)	SERVICE(S) COMPLETED	COMPLETED BY	WORK ORDER #

BOAT/MOTOR MAINTENANCE

BOAT MAKE		MODEL			
YEAR		HIN			
MOTOR MAKE		MODEL		SERIAL #	

DATE (MM/DD/YY)	ENGINE HOURS (P/S)	SERVICE(S) COMPLETED	COMPLETED BY	WORK ORDER #

BOAT/MOTOR MAINTENANCE

BOAT MAKE		MODEL			
YEAR		HIN			
MOTOR MAKE		MODEL		SERIAL #	

DATE (MM/DD/YY)	ENGINE HOURS (P/S)	SERVICE(S) COMPLETED	COMPLETED BY	WORK ORDER #

BOAT/MOTOR MAINTENANCE

BOAT MAKE		MODEL			
YEAR		HIN			
MOTOR MAKE		MODEL		SERIAL #	

DATE (MM/DD/YY)	ENGINE HOURS (P/S)	SERVICE(S) COMPLETED	COMPLETED BY	WORK ORDER #

BOAT/MOTOR MAINTENANCE

BOAT MAKE		MODEL			
YEAR		HIN			
MOTOR MAKE		MODEL		SERIAL #	

DATE (MM/DD/YY)	ENGINE HOURS (P/S)	SERVICE(S) COMPLETED	COMPLETED BY	WORK ORDER #

BOAT/MOTOR MAINTENANCE

BOAT MAKE		MODEL			
YEAR		HIN			
MOTOR MAKE		MODEL		SERIAL #	

DATE (MM/DD/YY)	ENGINE HOURS (P/S)	SERVICE(S) COMPLETED	COMPLETED BY	WORK ORDER #

BOAT/MOTOR MAINTENANCE

BOAT MAKE		MODEL			
YEAR		HIN			
MOTOR MAKE		MODEL		SERIAL #	

DATE (MM/DD/YY)	ENGINE HOURS (P/S)	SERVICE(S) COMPLETED	COMPLETED BY	WORK ORDER #

BOAT/MOTOR MAINTENANCE

BOAT MAKE		MODEL			
YEAR		HIN			
MOTOR MAKE		MODEL		SERIAL #	

DATE (MM/DD/YY)	ENGINE HOURS (P/S)	SERVICE(S) COMPLETED	COMPLETED BY	WORK ORDER #

BOAT/MOTOR MAINTENANCE

BOAT MAKE		MODEL			
YEAR		HIN			
MOTOR MAKE		MODEL		SERIAL #	

DATE (MM/DD/YY)	ENGINE HOURS (P/S)	SERVICE(S) COMPLETED	COMPLETED BY	WORK ORDER #

BOAT/MOTOR MAINTENANCE

BOAT MAKE		MODEL			
YEAR		HIN			
MOTOR MAKE		MODEL		SERIAL #	

DATE (MM/DD/YY)	ENGINE HOURS (P/S)	SERVICE(S) COMPLETED	COMPLETED BY	WORK ORDER #

NOTES

NOTES

NOTES

NOTES

NOTES

NOTES

NOTES

NOTES

NOTES

NOTES

NOTES

NOTES

NOTES

NOTES

NOTES

NOTES

NOTES

NOTES

NOTES

NOTES

Printed in Dunstable, United Kingdom

65344669R00067